TATTING
COLLAGE

TATTING
COLLAGE

LINDSAY ROGERS

Guild of Master Craftsman Publications Ltd

First published 1996 by
Guild of Master Craftsman Publications Ltd,
166 High Street, Lewes, East Sussex BN7 1XU

Reprinted 1998

ISBN 1 86108 020 4

Photography by Alex Gillespie LMPA
Illustrations by John Yates

The publishers and author can accept no legal responsibility for any
consequences arising from the application of information, advice or
instructions given in this publication.

Designed by Ed White
Typeface: Palatino

Printed and bound in Great Britain by
Redwood Books Limited, Trowbridge, Wiltshire

CONTENTS

INTRODUCTION

I first learned to tat as a child during the Second World War, taught by my mother's friend. Aged eight or nine at the time, I picked up the skill easily and was soon making myself smocked blouses with tatted edgings. Since then, I have always tatted to some extent, but only took it up on a more full-time basis in 1987, when I heard about the Ring of Tatters (*see* p.15).

I find it tremendously satisfying to be involved in bringing an old, traditional craft back into the modern world. It is simple and portable, you can take your tatting equipment anywhere, and it always attracts interested questions from onlookers!

Tatting is basically a handmade lace, with each stitch composed of two half-hitch knots. The single thread is looped and knotted with the aid of a small shuttle, and people are often amazed that so simple a technique can produce such intricate results. Traditionally used for doyleys and edging handkerchiefs or collars, there is much more that can be done with tatting with a bit of imagination.

At a trade fair in Birmingham I happened to leaf through a book on Japanese quilts and noticed a design of two superimposed trees. I just had to buy the book, and this was the beginning of my 'bonsai tree' designs (*see* p.65) and tatting collage pictures.

Tatting collage is an excellent way of making designs and pictures by assembling small pieces of tatting and gluing them down to card, paper or fabric. As well as offering great fun and flexibility, it also avoids the need to handle large and complicated pieces of tatting. This will be a welcome thought if you are pressed for time, or if you are fairly new to the craft and looking for encouragement. If you have only recently learned to tat, then completing some small pieces successfully will help you improve your skills and gain confidence.

Whatever your level of experience, this book offers the chance to create something satisfying and unique. This is not a book to teach you how to tat. I have assumed that readers will already be familiar with the basic techniques (other books explain the basic stitches very well – *see* Further Reading, p.85). Useful tips are given, however, in the Tools and Techniques section, and the section called How to Use this Book explains all you need to know about following the patterns and designs.

I have included some of the easiest tatting patterns possible, along with some more complex ones. The principles may be extremely simple, but the results can look wonderfully complicated and very attractive. Once you have got into the swing of putting your own designs together, you can give free rein to your imagination and develop your skills to create distinctive gifts and decorative pieces.

Lindsay

CHAPTER 1

A BRIEF HISTORY OF TATTING

ORIGINS

The origins of tatting are none too clear. It certainly evolved from knotting, an ancient means of making decorations for clothes and furnishings, similar to macramé. The word 'tatting', however, did not appear in print until the mid-nineteenth century.

Knotting was widely used in Europe from medieval times (no shuttle was used then, just fingers or a needle) and the craft developed in complexity until by the sixteenth century designs consisted of quite complicated loops, rings and connected rosettes. In the seventeenth century, knotting skills and techniques were given a further boost by Dutch trading connections with the Chinese, who used knotted threads extensively in their exquisite embroideries.

By this time the craft was highly fashionable in England. The ladies at the court of William and Mary, for example, were rarely seen without their shuttles (introduced to speed up the formation of knots). Shuttles were often highly elaborate and richly decorated – modern ones are smaller, and sadly plain by comparison! Tatting is a peaceful and elegant occupation, and the aristocracy liked to have their portraits painted while they showed off their hands using shuttle and thread.

DEVELOPMENT

Early examples of tatting show that it consisted largely of rings, sewn together afterwards, with no chains. Sometimes needleworked fillings were added to the centre of designs. Patterns tended to be passed down by word of mouth (or from hand to hand!) until the nineteenth century, when books about this popular craft began to be produced.

The grandly named Mademoiselle Eleonore Riego de la Branchardiere was an important figure in tatting history in the mid-1800s. She owned a lace and embroidery warehouse in London and published books of tatting patterns – eleven in all. Her method was to sew together tiny pieces, mostly rings, to create elaborate and intricate designs. She was the first to popularize the use of picots to sew the motifs together. She could even be said to have invented the 'wheel' – a central ring with picots forming a firm core for a larger design. It was not

FIG 1 A doyley made to a pattern by
Mlle Eleonore Riego de la Branchardiere, 1850.

until 1851, however, that an anonymous writer described a technique for joining the picots using a shuttle and crochet hook.

Fig 1 shows a typical design of that time, worked following one of Mademoiselle Riego's patterns. It was worked with a needle rather than a shuttle, and I used a linen floss thread which has an inconsistent thickness, just like the threads which would have been used in the nineteenth century. Fig 2 shows some examples of edging patterns from the 1860s.

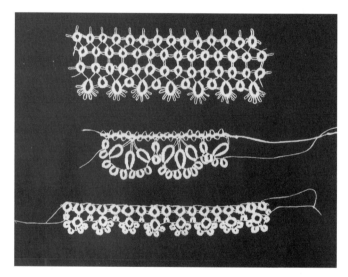

FIG 2 Samples of historical edging patterns.
Top: Etruscan border and insertion, 1861.
Centre: A simple edging with pearl beading, 1864.
Bottom: Oeillet edging, 1861.

THE TWENTIETH CENTURY

Tatting continued to be popular, with variations in style, into the early twentieth century. One landmark was the publication in 1910 of Lady Katherine Hoare's *The Art of*

Tatting, now something of a classic. Some of her illustrations and examples were taken from the work of Queen Elizabeth of Romania, an accomplished artiste who used richly decorated tatting in the beautiful pieces she made for the Church. (The Queen also wrote poetry and other works under the pen name of Carmen Sylva, and there was some mystery about the real identity of the writer.)

After the 1930s, however, tatting generally declined in popularity, although it seemed to keep a good following in America and Australia. It was also practised quite widely – although with variations – in Italy, Scandinavia, India and Japan.

Now that such crafts as bobbin lace are coming into vogue once again, I am glad to say that tatting is also being rediscovered. The equipment is minimal, cheap and highly portable, the techniques are simple to learn, and there is no limit to what can be accomplished!

CHAPTER 2

TOOLS AND TECHNIQUES

ESSENTIAL EQUIPMENT

You need very little special equipment for tatting:

- **Shuttle** – available from craft or haberdashery shops: there are many different types of shuttle, but they all do the same job, so choose what feels comfortable.
- **Small crochet hook**, e.g. 0.75mm.
- **Very sharp embroidery scissors**.
- **Lace maker's pricker** – useful for fraying tassels and for undoing tatting, something we all have to do from time to time.
- **The thread of your choice** – see below.

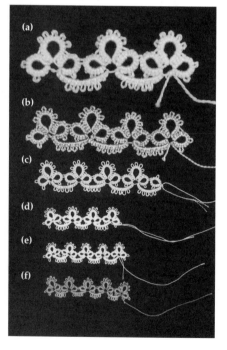

HANDY HINTS

THREAD

Thickness

All the examples illustrated in this book were worked with Coats no 60 crochet thread, but a nervous or inexperienced tatter could use the thicker no 20 with confidence, bearing in mind that the finished designs will be

FIG 3 The same pattern made with different threads.
(a) Mercerized crochet thread.
(b) Perle No 8.
(c) No 20.
(d) No 60.
(e) No 80.
(f) Sewing cotton.

slightly larger. Any thread can be used for tatting – literally anything from rope to sewing cotton! All that changes is the overall size and delicacy of the pattern, illustrated in Fig 3. It is important to choose something which will suit your purpose, however, and thread with a close twist and a smooth finish works best.

Keeping control of the ball thread

When working with ball and shuttle, there is nothing more irritating than having the ball of thread continually roll onto the floor. To prevent this, pull 2m (2yd) of thread from the ball and rewind firmly round the centre of the ball. Make a loop and twist the thread twice around itself,

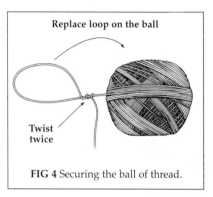

Replace loop on the ball

Twist twice

FIG 4 Securing the ball of thread.

replacing the loop on the ball (*see* Fig 4). By pulling the end of the thread in the right direction, more thread can be obtained easily. This method holds quite well. With a short thread leading to the work in progress, the added weight is also an aid to beginners struggling with tension.

CHAINS

When working a long chain for a flower stem or tree trunk it is a good idea to avoid the need to count large numbers of double stitches, as well as the havoc caused by interruptions. Work about half the required length, then hold the tatting in place on your picture and make a small mark on the shuttle thread with a pen. All you need do then is to continue making double stitches until the mark is reached.

Tension difficulties

The method just described also eliminates tension difficulties. Knots pushed close together make a shorter, stiffer chain, whereas loosely placed knots make a long, soft chain. The same number of knots can therefore make chains of quite different lengths and a tatter with a tight tension, for example, might find a set number of stitches too short for the pattern. Incidentally, leave the tension relaxed if a straight line is required, but push stitches close to go round corners.

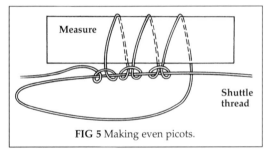

FIG 5 Making even picots.

EVEN PICOTS

To create large picots of even length when forming a fringe, for example, cut a stiff piece of plastic (the lid from a margarine tub is ideal) about 2in (5cm) long, with the width matching the size of picot required. When the picots are being made, the measure is held in the left hand, the thread forming the knot is passed round it and the shuttle makes the knot as normal (see Fig 5). The measure should slide out easily. You might like to keep the following measures to hand for use with this book: ¹/₈in (3mm), ¹/₄in (5mm), ³/₈in (1cm), ¹/₂in (1.3cm), 1in (2.5cm), 1¹/₂in (3.8cm), 2¹/₂in (6.5cm).

SECURING ENDS

Simple method

To secure the ends of the thread, tie half a reef knot, dab on a spot of glue, complete the knot and pull tight. When the glue is dry the ends can be cut so close that they hardly show.

Advanced method

For joins without knots, the following method will give a
professional neatness to your work. Avoid knotting the
ball and shuttle threads together at the start of a piece of
work. If the same colour is to be used, wind the shuttle
and begin tatting, leaving the thread attached to the ball.

If this is not possible, follow the method shown in
Fig 6. First work a ring, weaving the end into each half

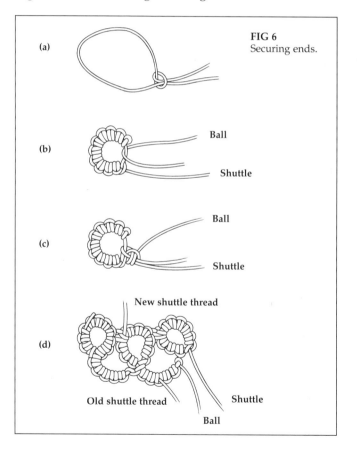

(a)

FIG 6
Securing ends.

(b)

Ball

Shuttle

(c)

Ball

Shuttle

(d)

New shuttle thread

Old shuttle thread

Shuttle

Ball

stitch as it is made (a), to lie alongside the shuttle thread or core. Three or four stitches will be sufficient. When the ring is complete, loop the ball thread through the base of the ring (b) and again work the unwanted end into the chain as part of the core (c). Throughout the course of a piece of work try to stagger the joins a little, as the two ends produced by one join will make the core thick and unsightly if woven in at the same time. This can be avoided by weaving one end into a ring and the other into a chain (d).

The best way

The best way to deal with ends is not to have any! Wherever possible use two balls of thread – one as the ball thread and the other to refill the shuttle when necessary. If this is not possible, however, and you have some thread left on the shuttle (but not quite enough to complete your design) and only one ball, loosely tie the threads together and finish filling the shuttle. Do not cut the thread, but work the design in the usual way using ball and shuttle. When you reach the knot on the shuttle, undo it and invisibly join in the ends as described above, continuing work with the thread remaining on the shuttle. This can avoid cutting the ball thread just to put a little more on the shuttle to finish a design.

MAKING THE COLLAGE

Preparation

It is wisest to work most of the pieces for a design before sticking anything down. If some pieces turn out to be unsuitable in the end, they can be kept for another project. A place can always be found for everything.

When each piece is completed, cover it with a damp cloth and press with a hot iron. This will flatten and stiffen the motif, making it much easier to handle and stick in place.

Equipment

A cocktail stick is useful for dabbing small amounts of glue onto the lace.

All-purpose PVA (polyvinyl acetate) adhesive is now widely available and will not cause the threads to rot or discolour. You can use whatever card or fabric suits your purpose for the collage, depending on whether you are making a card, a bookmark or something rather special to be framed. Anything goes: be adventurous. If you like the effect you have achieved, then it must be right!

THE RING OF TATTERS

If you are interested to learn more about tatting and to share ideas with likeminded people, why not join the Ring of Tatters? The Ring began in 1980 when a group of people attending a Tatting Course at the Devon Lace School decided to keep in touch. They produced a newsletter and things grew from there.

There is now an international membership of more than 1,500, although the Ring is still run on an informal basis by a team of volunteers. The annual subscription covers Spring and Autumn Newsletters, which include general articles, correspondence, patterns and details of books, suppliers and Tatting or Lace Days. A Register of Members is available for a small charge, so that local members can contact each other. There is also an extensive library of tatting books and patterns, although loans can only be made within the UK. The Ring is represented at craft shows and exhibitions, where their tatting demonstrations have promoted great interest in the craft, attracting many new members.

For membership details, please send a stamped, addressed envelope to:

The Membership Secretary,
Ring of Tatters,
269 Oregon Way,
Chaddesden,
Derby
DE21 6UR, England.

Please include an international reply coupon if you are writing from overseas.

CHAPTER 3

HOW TO USE THIS BOOK

USING THE PATTERNS

The main part of the book offers design ideas for tatting collage, from key rings and small cards to bookmarks and special occasion cards. The chapters begin by setting out patterns and instructions for making the motifs – single flowers, butterflies, etc. This is followed by a design section, with suggestions for the collage pictures which can be composed by putting the motifs together.

The individual patterns each have an identification number, for easy reference when putting a collage together. The letter (A–E) denotes the chapter, the number identifies the pattern within the chapter. For example, the small butterfly pattern is labelled A1, the dragonfly B15: instructions to put them together for a small card design would simply list the identification numbers alongside a picture of the collage. By the end of the book you will have a good number of individual patterns to mix and match just as you wish.

All pattern instructions are accompanied by a photograph of the finished piece and an 'exploded' diagram, showing the number and configuration of the stitches. A close look at both photograph and diagram before starting the piece is strongly recommended, especially for more complicated patterns.

FIG 7
Basic stitches

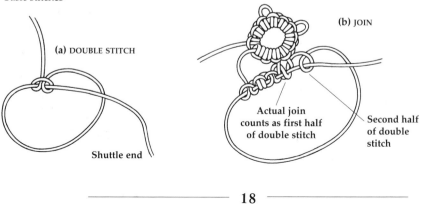

(a) DOUBLE STITCH

Shuttle end

(b) JOIN

Actual join counts as first half of double stitch

Second half of double stitch

ABBREVIATIONS

The following abbreviations are used in the pattern instructions.

ds double stitch
J join
cl close ring
p small picot for ornamentation or join
P large picot (sometimes a specific measurement is given)
rw reverse work (turn upside down)
* pattern worked with shuttle alone (creates rings)
** pattern worked with ball of thread and shuttle (creates rings and chains)

Note: It is almost always necessary to reverse the work between each ring and chain. This is such common practice that it is not always mentioned specifically in the patterns.

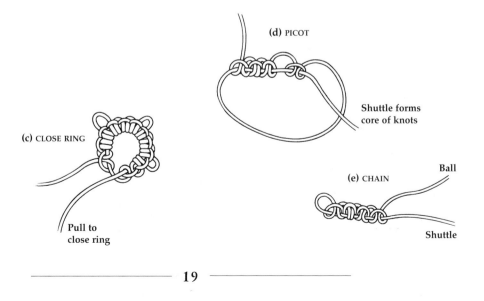

(d) PICOT

Shuttle forms
core of knots

(c) CLOSE RING

Ball

(e) CHAIN

Pull to
close ring

Shuttle

CHAPTER 4

STATIONERY, GIFT TAGS AND KEY RINGS

A Patterns

Patterns

These are some of the simplest tatted motifs. A single flower, cross or butterfly can make a very attractive key ring decoration, and all can be used to good effect on gift tags or notepaper for that special touch.

Small Butterfly

Front wing: *ring* – (6ds, p) x 3, 6ds, cl.
Rear wing: *ring* – (6ds, p) x 2, 6ds, cl.
Join these rings if you wish. Repeat rear wing, then front wing. Tie ends together and knot to form antennae.
For a tiny butterfly use 4ds only.

Butterfly

Front wing: *ring* – 10ds, (p, 2ds) x 7, 8ds, cl.
Rear wing: *ring* – 10ds, J, 10ds, p, 10ds, cl.
Repeat this wing, but do not join to the previous one. Make another front wing, tie threads together and knot for antennae.

Daisy

Flower: *ring* – 12P, cl.
Leave about ⅝in (1.5cm) thread for stalk.
Leaves: *ring* – 25ds, cl.
Make two leaves.

SMALL FLOWER

A4*

Ring – each petal 6ds, 3p, 6ds, cl.
Make five petals.

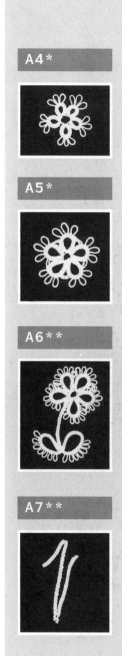

LARGE FLOWER

A5*

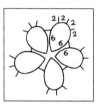

Ring – each petal 6ds, (p, 2ds) x 5, 4ds, cl.
Work five, six, or even seven petals, joining first and last p each time.

FLOWER AND LEAVES

A6**

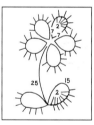

Flower: *ring* – each petal 7ds, p, (2ds, p) x 6, 7ds.
Make five petals, then join in ball thread.
Stalk: *chain* of 25ds.
Leaves: *ring* – (2ds, p) x 7, 15ds, cl.
Make two leaves.

TALL GRASS

A7**

Make a simple chain of a suitable length and, if required, fold the top over when sticking into place.

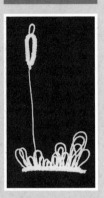

BULLRUSH

Ring – 12ds, P, 12ds, cl. Pull to long shape rather than round.
Leave a length of thread for stalk.

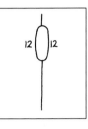

A9** GRASS

Make a series of Ps, or 2ds, P, of various lengths.

DUCK

Body: *ring* – 12ds, P, 20ds, cl.
Head: *ring* – 6ds, P, 6ds, cl.
Tie ends together and trim off.
Push body to oval shape and cut
P on head ring for beak.

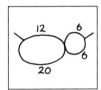

DANDELION

Head: *ring* – 1ds, 10P [¼in (5mm)], cl.
Leave 1in (2.5cm) thread for stalk.
Leaves: *ring* – 30ds, cl.
Make two leaves.
Cut picots of flower, fray out with
needle and trim tidy.

THISTLE

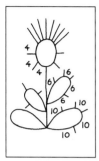

Head: *ring* – 4ds, (p, 4ds) x 2, 8P [¼in (5mm)], 4ds, (p, 4ds) x 2, cl.
Leave ½in (1.3cm) thread for stalk.
Leaves: *ring* – (6ds, p) x 3, 6ds, cl.
Make two leaves.
Lower leaves: *ring* – (10ds, p) x 3, 10ds, cl. Make two.

Note: For dandelion seed and thistledown tie a knot in a piece of thread about ¼in (5mm) from the end. Fray this thread with a lace maker's pricker or a needle and tidy to a suitable length before cutting just behind the knot (the seed). Stick in place before it gets lost!

FOXGLOVE

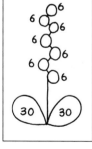

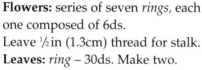

Flowers: series of seven *rings*, each one composed of 6ds.
Leave ½in (1.3cm) thread for stalk.
Leaves: *ring* – 30ds. Make two.

A14*

DELPHINIUM

Flowers: starting at the top, work
rings in pairs, each pair as follows:
6ds; 8ds; 10ds; 6ds, p, 6ds; 7ds, 2p,
7ds; 8ds, 3p, 8ds.
Leaves: *ring* – 18ds, (p, 2ds) x 3, 16ds.
Make three leaves.
Reverse work between each flower
ring to make finished design lie quite
flat.

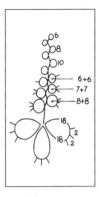

A15*

SPIDER

Head: *ring* – 10ds, cl.
Body: *ring* – 1ds, 2P [1in (2.5cm)],
10ds, 2P [1in (2.5cm)], cl.
Tie ends, cut picots for legs and bend
with your thumb nail.

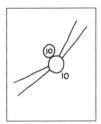

A16**

CROSS

Ring – (8ds, p) x 3, 8ds, cl. Make three.
Chain – 16ds.
Ring – (4ds, p) x 3, 4ds, cl.
Chain – 16ds.
Tie off and cut threads.

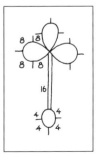

DESIGNS

The individual motifs described above can be put together in a collage, to make more elaborate decorations for stationery and so on. Some suggested collage designs are given below, with a list of their component parts, but why not try putting together your own from the motifs you like best?

A7, A8, A9, A10

A3, A7, A9, A13

A13

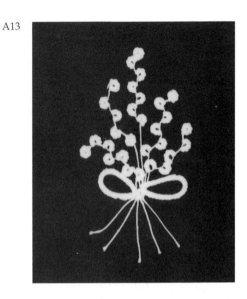

A3, A5, A7, A9,
½ of A2

A3, A9, A1
working 4ds
only

A11, A12
(dandelion seed)

A1, A3, Edging 1
(*see* Appendix)

CHAPTER 5

SMALL CARDS AND PAPERWEIGHTS

B Patterns

PATTERNS

For small cards or paperweight decorations, where there is a larger space to play with, more elaborate designs are possible. Below are some patterns to add to those given in the previous chapter.

In my experience, lace generally seems to be most acceptable worked in white, but the flower motifs particularly can be very attractive when coloured thread is used. Dark thread on brightly coloured card can also work well. Try a few experiments!

B1*

JOINED DAISES

Each flower: *ring* – 7p. Number of picots can vary, depending on size of flower required.
Leave ¼ in (5mm) thread between each ring.
For a more open flower work 2ds, p repeatedly.

B2*

CUT DAISY

Ring – 10p. Leave thread for stalk. Cut all picots to form an even circle and trim tidy.

POPPY

B3**

Centre: *ring* – 1ds, (3P, p) x 5, cl.
Tie in ball thread.
Petals: *chain* – (35ds, J to p) x 5.
Stalk: *chain* – 15ds, or more if required.

BUD

B4*

Ring – 9ds, p, 8ds, cl.
Ring – 8ds, J, (6ds, p) x 2, 8ds, cl.
Ring – 8ds, J, 9ds, cl.
Leave thread for stalk.

COMPOSITE LEAF

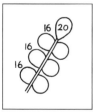

B5*

First four rings – 16ds.
Do not close these completely.
Fifth ring – 20ds, cl.
Sixth ring – 16ds, unclosed, J to fourth ring.
Seventh ring – 16ds, unclosed, J to third ring.
Eighth ring – 16ds, unclosed, J to second ring.
Ninth ring – 16ds, unclosed, J to first ring.

Variation: Make rings of 8ds, p, 8ds.

B6*

MULTI-HEAD THISTLE

Each head: *ring* – 8ds, 5P
[¼in (5mm)], 8ds, cl.
Work several on one stalk, cut all the
picots and fray with a needle. Tidy to
shape with very sharp scissors.

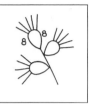

B7*

TOADSTOOLS

Head: large plain *ring*.
Stalk: smaller plain *ring*.
Secure ends and pull into shape when
pressing. Any toadstool shape can be
made in this way.

As a guide, toadstools with the
following ring sizes for head and stalk
are shown here: 50ds and 20ds; 30ds
and 10ds; 100ds and 30ds.

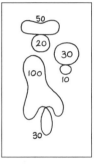

B8*

HAREBELL

Each flower: *ring* – 4ds, 3p, 4ds, cl.
Leave long thread for stalk.
For further flowers, work two rings
with long thread between them, and
tie onto first thread. More can be
added in the same way.

Note: This pattern can be adapted to
represent grass or oats by making
rings of 6ds, p, 6ds, cl.

CLOVER FLOWER

Inner ring – 3ds, (p, 2ds) x 5, 1ds, cl.
Join in ball thread.
Outer chain – 6ds, (p, 2ds) x 15, 4ds.
Tie to base of ring, but do not cut.
Stalk chain – 15ds or longer.

CLOVER LEAF

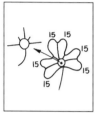

Centre: *ring* – 1ds,
(P [½in (1.3cm)], p) x 3, cl.
Leaves: *chain* – (15ds, J to twisted P,
15ds, J to p) x 3.
Tie off securely.
Stalk: *chain* – 15ds or longer.
Now try a four-leaf clover for luck!

SNAIL

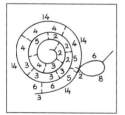

Start at the centre of the shell.
Chain – 1ds, p, 2ds, p, 3ds, p, 4ds,
p, 5ds, p, 2ds, J to 1st p, 2ds, p,
2ds, J, (3ds, p, 3ds, J) x 2, (4ds, p,
4ds, J) x 2, 5ds, p, 5ds, J, 6ds, p,
6ds, J, (14ds, J) x 3.
Head: *ring* – 6ds, P [2½in (6.5cm)],
8ds, cl.
Body: *chain* – 2ds, J to same p as
last J, 14ds, J, 3ds.
Finish tail neatly with a knot.
Cut and knot antennae.

OWL

Eye: *ring* – 6ds, p, 6ds, cl.
Head: *chain* – 3ds, p, 6ds, p, 3ds.
Eye: *ring* – 6ds, J, 6ds, cl.
Body: *chain* – 20ds, 2p, 3ds, 2p, 20ds.
Secure threads at first eye.

WREN

Head: *ring* – 9ds, p, 9ds, cl.
Body: *ring* – 12ds, 3P, 16ds, cl.
Cut p for beak.

BIRD OF PARADISE

As for Wren, but work very large Ps for tail.

DRAGONFLY

Head: *ring* – 12ds, cl.
Body: *ring* – 1ds, 2P (very large), 4ds,
p, 4ds, 2P, cl.
Do not cut thread.
Tail: pull shuttle thread through
p with crochet hook to form a 6in
(15cm) loop. Using shuttle as ball

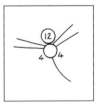

thread, work body with loop. Core to knots is therefore
two threads, making a thicker chain than normal.
Work 10ds and finish with a knot.

CROSS

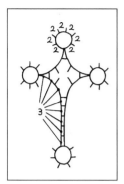

Ring – (2ds, p) x 6, 2ds, cl. rw.
Chain – (3ds, p) x 3, 3ds, rw.
Ring – as above.
Chain – 3ds, J, (3ds, p) x 2, 3ds, rw.
Ring – as above.
Chain – 3ds, J, (3ds, p) x 6, 3ds, rw.
Ring – as above.
Chain – (3ds, J) x 5, 3ds, p, 3ds, J, 3ds.
Tie threads.

DESIGNS

Use the patterns given in this chapter with those in the previous one to create designs for small cards or paperweights. The following illustrations may give you some ideas.

SMALL CARDS

A9, B1, B8

B3, B4, B5, small bud:
8ds, p, 8ds

A9, ½ of A2, B7, B11

A1 (4ds), B9, B10

A9, B8
(adapted), B14

B5, B12, plain chain for branch

PAPERWEIGHTS

Mounting a paperweight

Make a window template as shown in the diagram, cut out to the exact size of your glass paperweight, leaving a handle of card protruding for easy handling. Place the template on your chosen felt, with a weight on the handle if necessary, and stick the tatting pieces onto the felt inside the window. Remove the template. Dab glue onto the raised edge of the glass, place it over the design and weight down. When the glue is quite dry, trim off any excess felt.

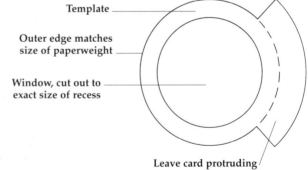

Template

Outer edge matches size of paperweight

Window, cut out to exact size of recess

Leave card protruding on one side as a handle

A7, A8, A9, B15

B1, centre ring:
(12ds) x 5

A3, A12

A6 with one leaf
(x2), A6 with
three petals only
and long stalk

CHAPTER 6

BOOKMARKS AND DOOR FINGER PLATES

C Patterns

Patterns

Bookmarks and door finger plates require a reasonable length of pattern to be effective, therefore tall grasses and 'continuation' designs often fit the bill. A shorter pattern can also very often be extended, for example with the addition of a butterfly or something similar.

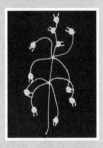

YORKSHIRE FOG GRASS

Seeds: *ring* – 3ds, p, 3ds, cl. Leave long thread for stalk. Cut picots. For further seeds, arrange on threads as for B8 (harebell).

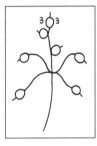

BUTTERFLY

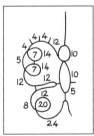

Head: *ring* – 10ds, P [2½ in (6.5cm)], 10ds, cl.
Body: *ring* – 10ds, p, (5ds, p) x 2, 10ds, cl. Tie with head, but do not cut off. Join in ball thread.
Front wing: *chain* – 12ds, (p, 4ds) x 3, rw; *ring* – 14ds, p, 7ds, cl, rw; *chain* – 5ds, rw; *ring* – 7ds, J to last ring, 14ds, cl, rw; *chain* – 12ds, p, 12ds, J to p on body ring.
Rear wing: *chain* – 12ds, J, 8ds, rw; *ring* – 20ds, cl, rw; *chain* – 24ds, J to second p of body ring.
For the other side of the butterfly, work these two wings in reverse and secure threads at head.

LARGE POPPY

Centre: *ring* – 1ds, (3P, p) x 5, cl.
Inner petals: *chain* – 30ds, J to p.
Make five petals.
Outer petals: *chain* – 45ds, J to p.
Make five petals.
Secure threads and make chain
for stalk.

C3*

POPPY BUD

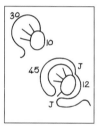

Ring – 1ds, 3P, p, 10ds, cl.
Chain – 30ds, J to p, rw.
Chain – 45ds, J to base of ring, 12ds,
finishing at p.
Work chain for stalk and, when
sticking down, overlap bud onto
stalk so that it 'grows' correctly.

C4*

LARGE HAREBELL

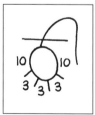

Flower: *ring* – 10ds, (p, 3ds) x 4, 7ds,
cl.
Leaves: *ring* – 1ds and pull up until
suitable size of leaf is achieved. A
spot of glue will stop this sliding out
of place.

C5*

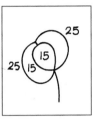

HAREBELL LEAF

Ring – 15ds, p, 15ds, cl.
Chain – 25ds, J, 25ds. Tie to base of leaf.

Note: Sizes of harebell flowers and leaves can be varied easily to fit your design.

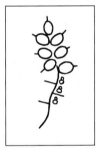

HEATHER

Flowers: series of *rings* – 6ds, p, 6ds; rw between each to make them lie flat.
Leaves and stems: these call for a slightly different technique to the familiar double stitch. On a chain, work the first half of the double stitch only, eight times, then P for leaves, followed by the second half of the double stitch, eight times, and another P. Repeat to whatever length required. This method twists the stem so that when the picots are cut to form the spiky leaves, they naturally lie on alternate sides of the stem. When leaves are no longer needed, continue working ½ds for a knobbly stem, or revert to the full ds for a smooth stem.

LARGE THISTLE

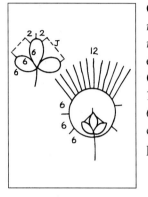

Centre: *ring* – 6ds, p, 6ds, cl; *ring* – 6ds, J, (2ds, p) x 2, 6ds, cl. *ring* – 6ds, J to last p, 6ds, cl. Tie ends and join in ball thread.
Outside: *chain* – (6ds, p) x 2, 6ds, 12P [³⁄₈ in (1cm)], (6ds, p) x 2, 6ds. Tie off and make plain chain for stalk. Cut and trim the picots.

BARLEY

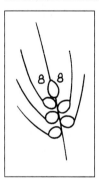

Each ring – 8ds, P [1½ in (3.8cm)], 8ds, cl. Work ten or twelve, rw between each one. Cut the picots and trim if necessary.

C10** | DAISY CHAIN

Petals: *ring* – 10ds, p, 5ds, (P, 2ds) x 3, 3ds, p, 10ds, cl. Make seven petals, joining first and last p of each.

Stalk: *chain* – 30ds.

Leaf: *chain* – (P, 2ds) x 14, 18ds, J to first P. Push stitches close for a curve and fold so they lie in the same direction as the picots.

Lower stalk: *chain* – 30ds, or more for the curl at the end.

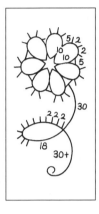

A7, A9, C1

DESIGNS

Bookmarks and door finger plates can both be made by adapting any of the patterns in this chapter. With my bookmarks, it can look as if the design is applied upside down, as the fringing appears at the top. It seems sensible to me, however, to keep the lace clean between the pages of the book, while a clear length of fringing marks the place.

You will find that it is sometimes necessary to take a bit of artistic licence, particularly when trying to make your chosen design fit into the long, narrow shape of a door finger plate or bookmark. This is no bad thing, however: it is called originality!

A3, A7,
A8, A9,
B15

HOW TO MAKE A BOOKMARK

Choose a coloured card or firm fabric as the base for the bookmark and simply stick down the tatting according to your planned design. Make a fringe at one end of the bookmark.

Other possible bookmark designs

A1, A9, C7

A12, C8

A3, A16

HOW TO MAKE A DOOR FINGER PLATE

If you have sticky fingered children around, this is an excellent way to add interest to something functional. Cut a piece of coloured card (or card covered with fabric to suit your decor) to fit the recess of a clear plastic door finger plate. These plates are obtainable from some craft shops or hardware shops. Arrange your tatting design and stick it down. Cover with the plastic finger plate and screw this to the door. I have been told that the plates should be put 'at the bottom for a Dachshund, at the top for a Great Dane and in the middle for children'!

Note: Of course, the designs for bookmarks and door finger plates are entirely interchangeable: any collage arranged to be long and thin will suit very well.

C10

B5, C3, C4

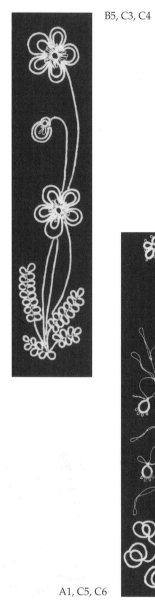

A7, A9, C9

A1, C5, C6

CHAPTER 7

FAVOURS AND DOLLS' HOUSE DOYLEYS

D Patterns

Patterns and Designs

A favour is a small token of affection or remembrance. These intricate and traditional designs are all beautiful by themselves, and are perfect for dolls' houses. Detailed patterns for each favour are given below. Some are also suitable for use in larger collages (*see* Chapter 9 for suggestions).

It is now possible to buy a wide variety of beautiful colours in fine crochet or tatting cotton. You might like to try these designs in two colours. Remember that if red, for example, is wound onto the shuttle, rings will appear red, because the knots are formed with this thread. If white is used from the ball to make a chain, knots will be white, as the red shuttle thread then forms the core to the knots.

D1 ★ ★

'TATTERED' HEART

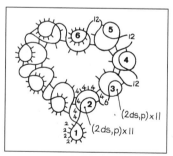

Start at base ring 1. All rings are the same.
Ring 1 – (2ds, p) x 11, 2ds, cl, rw.
Chain – 4ds. *Ring 2*, as above.
Chain – (4ds, p) x 5, 4ds, J to sixth p of ring, 6ds. *Ring 3*.
Chain – 4ds, J, (4ds, p) x 4, 4ds, J to sixth p of ring, 12ds. *Ring 4*.
Chain – (4ds, J) x 2, (4ds, p) x 3, 4ds, J to sixth p of ring, 12ds. *Ring 5*.
Chain – (4ds, J) x 2, (4ds, p) x 3, 4ds, J to sixth p of ring, 12ds. *Ring 6* – this is the central top ring.

Chain – 4ds, J to second p of last chain, (4ds, p) x 4, 4ds, J to sixth p of ring, 12ds. *Ring.*
Chain – 4ds, p, 4ds, J to last p of previous chain, (4ds, p) x 3, 4ds, J to sixth p of ring, 12ds. *Ring.*
Chain – (4ds, J) x 2, (4ds, p) x 3, 4ds, J to sixth p of ring, 12ds. *Ring.*
Chain – (4ds, J) x 2, (4ds, p) x 3, 4ds, J to sixth p of ring, 6ds. *Ring.*
Chain – 4ds, J, (4ds, p) x 2, (4ds, J) x 2 to ps on first chain, 4ds, J to sixth p of last ring, 4ds, J to base of first ring and secure ends.

Well done if you make it work first time!

CROSS

Start at left-hand trefoil.
Ring – (4ds, p) x 3, 4ds, cl.
Ring – 4ds, J, (4ds, p) x 2, 4ds, cl.
Ring – as above, rw. These three rings form the trefoil.
Chain – (4ds, p) x 3, 4ds, rw. Repeat trefoil.
Chain – 4ds, J, (4ds, p) x 2, 4ds, rw. Repeat trefoil.
Chain – 4ds, J, (4ds, p) x 6, 4ds, rw. Repeat trefoil.
Chain – (4ds, J) x 5, 4ds, p, 4ds, J, 4ds. Tie ends at first trefoil.

D3*

CELTIC CROSS

Start with the inner group of four rings.
Each ring – 6ds, p, (3ds, p) x 2, 6ds, cl. J first and third ps, rw.
Then make an outer group of six rings in the same way, rw at the end.

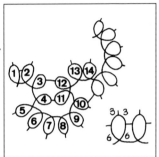

Make a second inner group of four rings. J first two rings with last two rings of the first group of four, at second ps. (If this seems like double Dutch, study the diagram and photograph very carefully.)

Continue until four groups of inner rings and four groups of outer rings are all joined up.

D4**

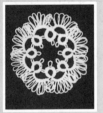

FRINGED DOYLEY

Each ring – (4ds, p) x 3, 4ds, cl.
Each chain – 8P [¼in (5mm)].
Work this ring and chain pattern eight times, joining first and last ps of all rings. Tie ends off at base of first ring.

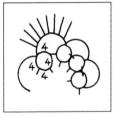

TREFOIL CROSS

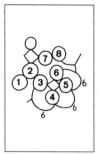

Start at a trefoil. All rings are the same.

Ring – 6ds, P, 6ds, cl. Make three rings to form a trefoil, rw.
Chain – 6ds, p, 6ds, rw.
Ring – 6ds, J to P of last ring, 6ds, cl, rw.
Chain – 6ds, rw.
Ring – as above, rw.
Chain – 6ds, p, 6ds, rw.

Work another trefoil and repeat the whole sequence until the square is formed.

TASSEL FLOWER

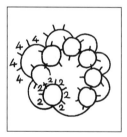

Ring – (2ds, p) x 5, 2ds, cl, rw.
Chain – (4ds, p) x 3, 4ds.
Work this sequence seven times, J second and fourth ps of rings except the last time. Complete the last chain and J to first ring.
Tassel: wind thread 50 times round a matchbox or something of similar size, cut once and remove.

Fold these threads over the open chain and bind with an extra thread, tying firmly.

OVAL DOYLEY

Outer rings – 4ds, (p, 2ds) x 5, 2ds, cl, rw.
Inner rings – (4ds, p) x 3, 4ds, cl, rw.
J first and last ps of both inner and outer rings.
J centre ps also when working second side of doyley.
Five outer rings close together make the rounded ends.
This design can be extended for a table runner.

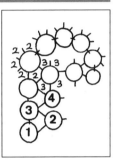

SQUARE MAT

Centre: *ring* – (4ds, p) x 5, 4ds, cl.
Make four, J first and last p.
Tie off ends.
Outer row: *ring* – 4ds, p, 4ds, J to second p of a centre ring, 4ds, p, 4ds, cl, rw;
chain – (2ds, p) x 5, 2ds, rw. All chains are the same;
ring – 4ds, J to first ring of this row, 4ds, J to second centre ring, 4ds, p, 4ds, cl, rw;
chain – as above;
ring – 4ds, p, 4ds, J to last free p of centre ring, 4ds, p, 4ds, cl, rw.
Continue until square is completed and secure ends.

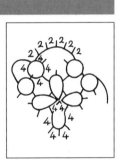

EIGHT-RING SNOWFLAKE

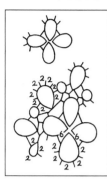

Centre: *ring* – 6ds, (P, 2ds) x 6, 4ds, cl. Make four rings, J first and last P all round.

Outer row: *ring* – (2ds, p) x 7, 2ds, cl. J to second P of centre row; *small ring* – 2ds, J to last p of last ring, 2ds, p, 2ds, cl. J to third P of centre row; *ring* – 2ds, J to small ring, (2ds, p) x 6, 2ds, cl. J to fourth P of centre row; *small ring* – as above, J to fifth P of centre ring. Continue to complete the circle and tie off ends.

Variation: Make five rings at the centre and therefore ten outer rings for a more impressive snowflake. These can be starched and hung on a Christmas tree.

BUTTERFLY

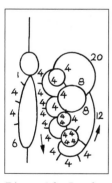

Each wing is worked separately. Start at base of large ring:
Ring – 4ds, p, (8ds, p) x 2, 4ds, cl, rw.
Chain – 4ds, p, 4ds, rw.
Ring – 4ds, J, 4ds, p, 4ds, cl, rw.
Chain – as above.
Ring – 4ds, J, (4ds, p) x 2, 4ds, cl, rw.
Chain – (4ds, p) x 2, 4ds, J to last p of last ring, 12ds, J to middle p of first ring, 20ds, rw.

Ring – 4ds, J to last p of first ring, 4ds, cl, rw.
Chain – 4ds, p, 4ds. Tie off threads.
Make two wings.
Head: *ring* – 8ds, P [2½in (6.5cm)], 8ds, cl.

Body: *ring* – 1ds, J to wing, (4ds, J) x 2, 6ds, p, 6ds, J to second wing (take care to get this the right way round!), 4ds, J, 4ds, J, 1ds. Secure ends at head. Cut and knot antennae.

RINGED THISTLE

Thistle: *ring* – (6ds, p) x 3, 6ds, cl, rw; *chain* – 6ds, J, (3ds, p, 3ds, J) x 2, 6ds, J to base of ring; *chain* – (4ds, p) x 3, 4ds, J, 10P [³⁄₈in (1cm)], J, (4ds, p) x 3, 4ds, J to base of ring.
Stalk: *chain* – 12ds.
Leaves: *ring* – 10ds, p, 6ds, nearly cl. Repeat; *end ring* – 10ds, p, 10ds, cl; *ring* – 6ds, p, 10ds, nearly cl, J at second ring.

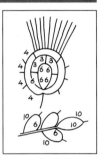

Repeat, J at first ring. Repeat again. 1ds on ball thread, then make a second leaf.
Complete stalk with 6ds, and tie off with a knot.

SNOWFLAKE

Ring – 4ds, p, (2ds, p) x 4, 4ds, cl.
Ring – 4ds, J, (2ds, p) x 4, 4ds, cl.
Ring – as above, rw. This makes the trefoil.
Chain – (4ds, p) x 3, 4ds, rw. Repeat trefoil.
Chain – 4ds, J, (4ds, p) x 2, 4ds, rw. Repeat trefoil.
Work this sequence until five trefoils are completed, J last chain to first.

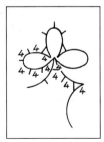

DOG ROSE

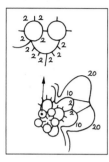

Start at centre of flower.
Ring – (2ds, p) x 3, 2ds, cl, rw.
Chain – (2ds, p) x 2, 2ds, P ['/8 in (3mm)], (2ds, p) x 2, 2ds, rw. Work this sequence five times, J at first and third ps all round. Do not fasten thread, but continue to petals.
Chain – 10ds, P ['/4 in (5mm)], 2ds, J to P of previous chain, 2ds, P ['/4 in (5mm)], 10ds, J between chains of last row.
Chain – 20ds, J to 2Ps together of previous row, 20ds, J between chains of last row.
Stalk: *chain* – 15ds.
Leaf: *ring* – 10ds, p, 5ds, cl to '/8 in (3mm). Repeat; *ring* – 10ds, p, 10ds, cl tightly; *ring* – 5ds, p, 10ds, cl to '/8 in (3mm), J between first two rings. Repeat this ring and chain, 3ds, then make another leaf and finish with stalk of 10ds.

Note: Work this design in no 80 thread to fit a paperweight.

FOUR-LEAF CLOVER

See B10 for instructions on working a four-leaf clover.
Add stalk of 15ds.
Small ring – 6ds, 3p, 6ds, cl.
Then make another stalk and the second clover leaf.
Secure ends. See B9 for instructions on working a clover flower.
Add stalk of 15ds and secure ends at small ring between leaf stalks.

Note: This design looks very pretty at the edge of a bridal veil or dress. Such a design could also include one of the butterfly patterns.

D15**

AUTUMN LEAF

Ring – (3ds, p) x 3, 3ds, cl, rw.
Chain – (2ds, p) x 3, 2ds, rw.
Ring – 5ds, J, (5ds, p) x 2, 5ds, cl, rw.
Chain – (2ds, p) x 5, 2ds, rw.
Ring – 7ds, J, (7ds, p) x 2, 7ds, cl, rw.
Chain – (2ds, p) x 7, 2ds, rw.
Ring – 7ds, J, (7ds, p) x 2, 7ds, cl, rw.
Chain – (2ds, p) x 5, 2ds, rw.

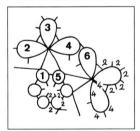

Ring – 5ds, J, (5ds, p) x 2, 5ds, cl, rw.
Chain – (2ds, p) x 4, ¹/₂ds worked wrongly to lock thread, rw.
Chain – 5ds, J to last p of last ring, 5ds, J to same ring, (4ds, J) x 4, 4ds.
Ring – 4ds, J, 8ds, cl, rw.
Chain – 30ds, J, ¹/₂ds to lock, 20ds drawn tight to curl.
Finish off with a knot.

D16*

WEB SNOWFLAKE

Small ring – (2ds, p) x 3, 2ds, cl, rw. Leave ¹/₄in (5mm) thread.
Ring – (4ds, p) x 3, 4ds, cl.
Ring – 4ds, J, (2ds, p) x 5, 4ds, cl.
Ring – 4ds, J, (4ds, p) x 2, 4ds, cl, rw. Leave ¹/₄in (5mm) thread.
Repeat this sequence, J all small rings at first and last ps, J trefoils at middle ps of first and last rings.

ROSE WINDOW

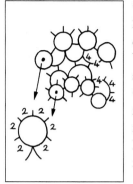

Centre row: *ring* – (2ds, p) x 5, 2ds, cl, rw. All rings are the same; *chain* – (4ds, p) x 2, 4ds, rw. Work this sequence seven times, J second and fourth ps of the rings. **Outer row:** *rings* – as above, J first and fifth ps; *chain* – 4ds, J to first row chain, 4ds, rw. Repeat this sequence to J with first ring. Tie off.

CHAPTER 8

BONSAI TREE PICTURES

E Patterns

PATTERNS

Embroiderers often include flowers in their designs, and tatted flower motifs have also featured largely in previous chapters of this book. Why not extend this to trees?

Most designs in this chapter are composed of, or adapted from, patterns given previously. Some small motifs especially suitable for tree pictures will be new, however, and instructions for these are given below.

PINE NEEDLES

Chain – 6ds.
Ring – 1ds, 2P, cl.
Continue along the branch in this way, making Ps quite long for the needles – you can cut them shorter, but they can't be lengthened later!

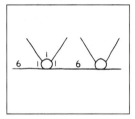

VINE LEAF

Ring – (2ds, P [¹/₈in (3mm)]) x 2, 2ds, cl.
Chain – 9ds, p, 5ds, J, 7ds, p, 7ds, J, 5ds, p, 9ds. Tie ends.

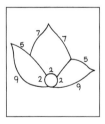

GRAPES

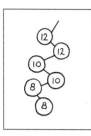

E3*

Start at the bottom of the bunch and make pairs of rings. First pair – 8ds; second – 10ds; third – 12ds.
Take care to hang them vertically, with the stalk at the top, when sticking down!

PALM LEAF

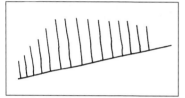

E4**

Worked in the same way as grass (see A9), but take care here because the lengths of the picots shape the leaf.

BAMBOO

E5*

Make a ring of three long Ps. Additional leaves as for harebell (C5). The secret is to stick them down carefully with the aid of a needle to pull the points tight. This motif works well in Japanese-style pictures.

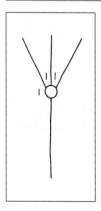

JOSEPHINE KNOTS

Each ring is formed using $\frac{1}{2}$ds only. This makes tiny buds which are very neat and flat. Try making them with $\frac{1}{2}$ds x 6, 8 or 10.

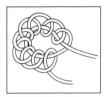

DESIGNS

Bonsai trees are small, attractive and unusual, but these pictures are not difficult to make. If you want to branch out on your own, take a careful look at your favourite tree in the garden, photograph or sketch it, simplify the outline and then make it in tatting. Whether following the designs suggested below or making your own, always start at the tips of the branches, working towards and then down the trunk. The trunks and branches are just plain chains, worked to the desired length.

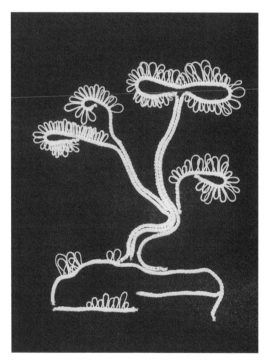

Tree on a rock
Work leaves similar to grass, A9. Use plain chains to 'draw' the rest of the picture.

Cedar tree
E1, E5

Grape vine
E2, E3

Palm tree
E4. Coconuts are
simply plain rings.

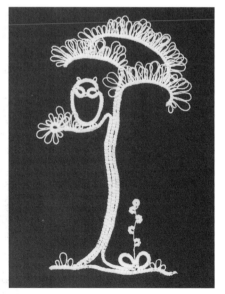

Scots pine
Leaves as grass,
A9. A13, B12.

Japanese apple tree
A5, E5, E6.

Japanese cherry tree
Rings – (2ds, p) x 3,
2ds, cl. (similar to
daisies, B1).
Join ball thread to
last flower to work
branches and trunk.

CHAPTER 9

SPECIAL OCCASION CARDS

IDEAS FOR LARGER DESIGNS

By this time you will be familiar with all the abbreviations in the patterns and with the necessary techniques for basic tatting. There is really no limit to what can be created with a tatting shuttle and a ball of thread. Now is the time to let your imagination run free and start designing more complicated pieces of collage.

Making quite sizeable cards of tatting collage can be a unique way of marking a special occasion, perhaps an important birthday, or a particular event such as a wedding. You can guarantee that your card will stand out from the crowd!

The following suggestions can, of course, be freely adapted to suit your needs and preferences. Simply put motifs together to make the picture you want. With a bit of careful thought, many of the patterns can also be adapted to suit the sizing you require.

Have fun!

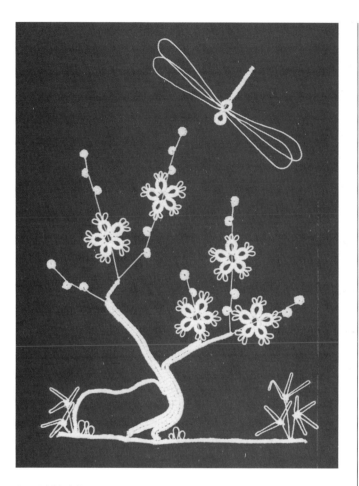

Special birthday
A4, B15, E5, E6.

Musical celebration
B1, B6, B8, B14. For the treble clef, work a long chain and
pull stitches close for the curves, loose for the straight parts.

Wedding
B6, B13, B14, C7, D1.

Confirmation
A3, A4, A5, B8, D2.

Spider's web design
A3, A5, A7, A15, B8.
When sticking a single thread of some length, glue the tip and weight it down, then pull straight, lightly glue the underside and press into place.

Birds and spider
A10 (double number of ds), B13.
Spider – 3ds, P (for legs), 10ds, P, 3ds, cl.

Highland glen
A3, A13, B7. Bushes as for grass, A9.

Any occasion
Daisy chain, C10 (x2), D6 (without tassel).
Stems as in heather, C7.

Victorian posy
A4, A5, B2, Edging 1 (see Appendix).

APPENDIX: EDGINGS

Some people find creating a simple edging rather tedious; others find the repetitive work soothing and relaxing. Repetition is certainly a good way of getting the feel of tatting, and as confidence grows, improvement in technique can also be seen. A smart edging can be the making of an otherwise simple arrangement, and adds an elegant finishing touch. There are countless edging patterns given in other books on tatting, but here are two of my most versatile favourites. Both can form the basis of many variations.

EDGING 1

Ring 1 – (4ds, p) x 3, 4ds, cl, rw.
Chain – 4ds, p, 4ds, rw.
Ring 2 – 4ds, J, (4ds, p) x 2, 4ds, cl, rw.
Repeat sequence as necessary.

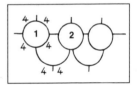

EDGING 2

Ring 1 – (4ds, p) x 3, 4ds, cl.
Ring 2 – 4ds, J, (2ds, p) x 6, 4ds, cl.
Ring 3 – 4ds, J, (4ds, p) x 2, 4ds, cl, rw.
Chain – 4ds, p, (2ds, p) x 4, 4ds, rw.
Repeat sequence, always J second p of fourth ring to second p of third ring.

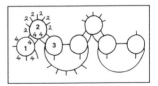

FURTHER READING

The Complete Book of Tatting by Rebecca Jones (Batsford, Dryad Press, 1985) is an excellent all-round reference book, explaining various tatting techniques in clear detail.

The Art of Tatting by Lady Katherine Hoare is also well worth reading if you can get hold of a copy. First published in 1910, there have been subsequent editions, although sadly none are in print at present.

For basic instructions, I recommend the following two publications:

Tatting (Coats Crafts UK, 1995) is a useful, all-round book, covering the basics of tatting, together with patterns for motifs, edgings and collars.

Learn Tatting by Rosemarie Peel (Lacet Publications, 1994) is a colour broadsheet folded to A5 size, showing in clear diagrams everything a beginner needs to know.

You should be able to obtain these publications from needlework shops, bookshops, or libraries. Tatting and Learn Tatting are also available from Garry Crafts, Invergarry, Inverness-shire, Scotland PH35 4HG.

About the Author

Lindsay Rogers has been interested in tatting and embroidery since childhood. She inherited a creative flair and an eye for design from her father, who was a successful professional artist. Much of the inspiration for her work comes from a lifetime of country living, first in Kent and then in Scotland, where she has lived with her husband since 1968. In 1978 they set up a craft shop in the village of Invergarry, to cater for the many visitors to their part of the Highlands, and Garry Crafts has become well known and loved.

Tatting has been a longstanding hobby for Lindsay, but her involvement grew once she had joined the Ring of Tatters in 1987. She now sells a wide variety of work through Garry Crafts and is increasingly sought out by individuals and other commercial concerns for help with design and techniques. She is also developing links in Japan, where tatting is a popular craft, and some of her work has been exhibited there.

TITLES AVAILABLE FROM

GMC PUBLICATIONS

BOOKS

￼OODWORKING

￼ Woodworking Plans & Projects	*GMC Publications*
￼es and Feeders for the Garden	*Dave Mackenzie*
￼te Woodfinishing	*Ian Hosker*
￼Woodwork	*Jeremy Broun*
￼re & Cabinetmaking Projects	*GMC Publications*
￼re Projects	*Rod Wales*
￼re Restoration (Practical Crafts)	*Kevin Jan Bonner*
￼re Restoration and Repair for Beginners	*Kevin Jan Bonner*
￼Woodwork	*Mike Abbott*
￼redible Router	*Jeremy Broun*
￼& Modifying Woodworking Tools	*Jim Kingshott*
￼Chairs and Tables	*GMC Publications*
￼Fine Furniture	*Tom Darby*

Making Little Boxes from Wood	*John Bennett*
Making Shaker Furniture	*Barry Jackson*
Pine Furniture Projects for the Home	*Dave Mackenzie*
The Router and Furniture & Cabinetmaking	
Test Reports	*GMC Publications*
Sharpening Pocket Reference Book	*Jim Kingshott*
Sharpening: The Complete Guide	*Jim Kingshott*
Space-Saving Furniture Projects	*Dave Mackenzie*
Stickmaking: A Complete Course	*Andrew Jones & Clive George*
Veneering: A Complete Course	*Ian Hosker*
Woodfinishing Handbook (Practical Crafts)	*Ian Hosker*
Woodworking Plans and Projects	*GMC Publications*
The Workshop	*Jim Kingshott*

￼OODTURNING

￼ures in Woodturning	*David Springett*
￼rsh: Woodturner	*Bert Marsh*
￼es' Notes from the Turning Shop	*Bill Jones*
￼es' Further Notes from the Turning Shop	*Bill Jones*
￼ng Techniques for Woodturners	*Jan Sanders*
￼aftsman Woodturner	*Peter Child*
￼ive Techniques for Woodturners	*Hilary Bowen*
￼al Tips for Woodturners	*GMC Publications*
￼te Turning	*GMC Publications*
￼the Lathe	*R.C. Bell*
￼ed Woodturning Techniques	*John Hunnex*
￼diate Woodturning Projects	*GMC Publications*
￼owley's Woodturning Projects	*Keith Rowley*
￼oney from Woodturning	*Ann & Bob Phillips*
￼entre Woodturning	*Ray Hopper*
￼ and Profit from Woodturning	*Reg Sherwin*

Practical Tips for Turners & Carvers	*GMC Publications*
Practical Tips for Woodturners	*GMC Publications*
Spindle Turning	*GMC Publications*
Turning Miniatures in Wood	*John Sainsbury*
Turning Wooden Toys	*Terry Lawrence*
Understanding Woodturning	*Ann & Bob Phillips*
Useful Techniques for Woodturners	*GMC Publications*
Useful Woodturning Projects	*GMC Publications*
Woodturning: A Foundation Course	*Keith Rowley*
Woodturning: A Source Book of Shapes	*John Hunnex*
Woodturning Jewellery	*Hilary Bowen*
Woodturning Masterclass	*Tony Boase*
Woodturning Techniques	*GMC Publications*
Woodturning Tools & Equipment Test Reports	*GMC Publications*
Woodturning Wizardry	*David Springett*

WOODCARVING

..ove represents a full list of all titles currently published or scheduled to be published. All are available direct from ..blishers or through bookshops, newsagents and specialist retailers. To place an order, or to obtain a complete ..gue, contact:

GMC Publications, 166 High Street, Lewes, East Sussex BN7 1XU United Kingdom
Tel: 01273 488005 Fax: 01273 478606

Orders by credit card are accepted